DEC 3 0 2019

SPECIAL FORCES OPERATOR

BY CHRIS BOWMAN

BELLWETHER MEDIA · MINNEAPOLIS · MN

TM

Are you ready to take it to the extreme?
Torque books thrust you into the action-packed world
of sports, vehicles, mystery, and adventure. These books
may include dirt, smoke, fire, and dangerous stunts.
WARNING: read at your own risk.

Library of Congress Cataloging-in-Publication Data

Bowman, Chris, 1990- author.
  Special Forces Operator / by Chris Bowman.
      pages cm -- (Torque: Dangerous Jobs)
  Summary: "Engaging images accompany information about Special Forces operators. The combination of high-interest subject matter and light text is intended for students in grades 3 through 7"-- Provided by publisher.
  Audience: Ages 7-12.
  Audience: Grades 3 to 7.
  Includes bibliographical references and index.
  ISBN 978-1-62617-114-5 (hbk. : alk. paper)
  1. Special forces (Military science)--United States--Juvenile literature. 2. United States--Armed Forces--Commando troops--Juvenile literature. I. Title.
  UA34.S64B6576 2013
  356'.160973--dc23
                            2013051262

TABLE OF CONTENTS

CHAPTER 1

QUICK STRIKE!

A team of twelve **Special Forces** operators sneaks up to an old house. They know that an enemy leader is hiding there. The team surrounds the house.

The soldiers run into the house. They have caught the enemy by surprise! They arrest him. Then they slip quietly back into the night. The city is safer thanks to these brave soldiers.

Powerful Allies

Army Special Forces is just one unit of special operations in the United States military. Other units include the Army Rangers, Army Delta Force, Navy SEALs, and Air Force Special Tactics.

CHAPTER 2

SPECIAL FORCES OPERATORS

Special Forces operators are highly trained soldiers in the United States Army. They take on secret **missions** in countries at war. They work undercover to gather information. They also teach others how to fight. These soldiers reach out to **foreign** peoples. They show that the U.S. is their friend.

A Symbol of Excellence

The Army Special Forces is also called the Green Berets. They earn this name from their hats. Their unique look sets them apart from other U.S. soldiers.

The Army Special Forces have many duties. Soldiers gather information on **reconnaissance** missions. They carry out **direct action strikes** against dangerous enemies. On **unconventional warfare** missions, they train foreign soldiers. Special Forces soldiers also stop **terrorists** from hurting innocent people.

A Special Group

Special Forces operators work in teams of 12 soldiers.

- Commanding Officer
- Warrant Officer
- Non-Commissioned Officer in Charge
- Operations and Intelligence Sergeant
- 2 Communications Sergeants
- 2 Engineer Sergeants
- 2 Medical Sergeants
- 2 Weapons Sergeants

Special Forces operators first complete **basic training**. Then they learn survival skills. They are trained in weapons and **navigation**. They also practice surviving enemy capture. Some teams learn to SCUBA dive. Others learn to jump from airplanes. Each person must learn a foreign language. They also learn how to teach other soldiers. Soldiers must pass every step to become Special Forces operators.

The Deep End

Soldiers who focus on diving even learn to dive without air tanks. They practice 50-foot (15-meter) dives!

M-4
Carbine

Stick to Your Guns

A Special Forces operator's main guns are the M-4 Carbine and the M9 Pistol. These light guns can be used in many kinds of jobs.

Special Forces operators use the best gear around. They have **night-vision goggles** to see in the dark. Kayaks, **inflatable** boats, and helicopters help them travel quickly and quietly. Those who jump from planes use **HALO helmets**. These help them breathe in the thin air. Soldiers who dive use **re-breathers** to swim undetected.

CHAPTER 3
DANGER!

Special Forces operators face constant danger. Because they are highly trained, they complete extremely dangerous missions. They are at a high risk to be injured or killed by the enemy. They also face unseen dangers. **IEDs** hide in the war zones where they work.

The soldiers always risk equipment failure. It could mean death on an airplane jump or a dive. Special Forces operators often work in enemy land. Training local soldiers can be unsafe. They usually do not have other soldiers nearby to help them if they get in trouble.

Out of Uniform

Certain laws protect soldiers who are captured during a war. However, they only apply to soldiers in uniform. Special Forces soldiers often wear normal clothes to blend in. This means they may be hurt or killed by the enemy if they are caught.

Special Forces operators risk their lives behind enemy lines. Despite the danger, they think their job is worth it. Many value the sense of belonging they feel with their fellow soldiers. Others love the responsibility of protecting their country. They are proud to be some of the best soldiers in the world.

Tragedy on the Job

On November 13, 2013, Staff Sergeant Richard Vazquez was killed while serving in Afghanistan. His Special Forces unit was on patrol when it was attacked with an IED. Vazquez died of injuries he received from the blast.

Glossary

basic training—the combination of drills, tests, and military training that all newly enlisted members of the United States Army must go through

direct action strikes—quick attacks

foreign—from another country

HALO helmets—helmets that have an air supply so soldiers can breathe at extreme heights; HALO stands for High Altitude, Low Opening.

IEDs—homemade bombs; IED stands for Improvised Explosive Device.

inflatable—able to be filled with air or gas

missions—military tasks

navigation—finding one's way in unfamiliar terrain

night-vision goggles—special sets of glasses that allow Special Forces operators to see at night

re-breathers—devices that help Special Forces operators breathe underwater

reconnaissance—gathering information about the enemy

Special Forces—military units that are specially trained in unconventional warfare; Special Forces teams often take on high-risk missions.

terrorists—people who perform violent acts to create fear among people

unconventional warfare—training forces in enemy-held land

To Learn More

AT THE LIBRARY

Alvarez, Carlos. *Army Delta Force*. Minneapolis, Minn.: Bellwether Media, 2010.

Loria, Laura. *Marine Force Recon*. New York, N.Y.: Gareth Stevens Pub., 2012.

Newman, Patricia. *Army Special Forces: Elite Operations*. Minneapolis, Minn.: Lerner Pub. Co., 2014.

ON THE WEB

Learning more about Special Forces operators is as easy as 1, 2, 3.

1. Go to www.factsurfer.com.

2. Enter "Special Forces operators" into the search box.

3. Click the "Surf" button and you will see a list of related web sites.

With factsurfer.com, finding more information is just a click away.

Index

The images in this book are reproduced through the courtesy of: Stockstrek Images/ SuperStock, front cover, pp. 20-21; Adam Ziaja, pp. 4-5, 6-7; United States Department of Defense, pp. 8-9, 10, 11, 12, 13, 14, 15, 18-19; BPTU, pp. 16-17.